W9-AYA-574

POLES APART

PIONEER EDITION

By Dolores Johnson and Michael E. Ruane

CONTENTS

Over 100 years ago, African American explorer Matthew Henson did what no one had ever done before. He braved cold and ice. He also faced racism. But in the end, he reached the North Pole.

ARCTI
ADVENTURER

By Dolores Johnson

Author of National Geographic's book *Onward*

Matthew Henson drove his sled over the ice. The **North Pole** was so close. It was April 1909. Suddenly the ice cracked. Henson, his dogs, and the sled fell into the Arctic Ocean. Would he ever reach the North Pole?

Ice Dangers

Explorers had tried to reach the North Pole before. They all failed. The trip was hard. Ice ridges could be taller than six-story buildings. Temperatures fell to minus 50° Celsius (minus 59° Fahrenheit).

The weather was warmer that April day. The ice had already started to thaw. It cracked. Now travel was even more risky. Henson kept going.

The Journey Begins

Henson's dream began 18 years earlier. That's when engineer Robert Peary hired him. Henson soon became his main helper.

Peary planned his first trip to the **Arctic Circle** in 1891. He needed Henson's help. Peary wondered if an African American could stand the cold. "I'll stand it as well as any man," Henson told him.

The journey began. Henson built sleds on the trip. He hunted and cooked. He also did other jobs. Henson and Perry dreamed of becoming famous explorers. Henson wanted to make all African Americans feel proud.

Rough Going. *The men traveled over rough ice (below). They wore special snowshoes (right). These helped the men stay on top of the snow.*

Survival Skills

On their way to the North Pole, the **expedition** members stayed with the Inuit people in Greenland. Henson learned their language.

The Inuit taught Henson how to survive in the Arctic. He learned to build houses from ice. They are called igloos. The Inuit made him warm clothes. They also taught him how to drive dogsleds.

Facing Setbacks

Peary led seven trips to the Arctic from 1891 to 1906. He faced many dangers each time. Sleds broke. Dogs died. Men got hurt.

Each trip took Peary and Henson closer to the North Pole. Yet they never reached it. So they tried one last time in 1908.

Peary, Henson, and six others set sail on July 6, 1908. They anchored at Cape Sheridan, Canada. It is 665 kilometers (413 miles) south of the North Pole. They built a team there.

The group of 24 men had 19 sleds. They also had 133 dogs. They brought meat, biscuits, and tea. They packed meat and animal fat for the dogs.

Arctic Outfit. *Henson wore a fur suit sewn by Inuit women.*

Tracing His Steps. *This map shows the route Henson followed to reach the North Pole.*

NORTH POLE

ARCTIC OCEAN

Cape Sheridan

GREENLAND

ARCTIC CIRCLE

ATLANTIC OCEAN

CANADA

UNITED STATES

New York

5

Final Try for the Pole

Peary's team began their last try for the Pole in late February 1909. By early April, they only had 214 kilometers (133 miles) to go. Peary told Henson and four Inuit to go ahead. He sent most of the other men back. It would save food.

Henson traveled up to 40 kilometers (25 miles) a day. All went well. Then he fell into the water. Ootah, an Inuit, saved him. Henson was wet and cold. But his dream was still alive! The Pole was within reach.

Farthest North

It was April 5, 1909. Peary checked his sextant. That is a **navigation** tool. The North Pole was just 56 kilometers (35 miles) away! He sent Henson ahead again.

Henson pushed on. He didn't stop. Finally he thought he had reached the Pole. Peary arrived soon after. "I think I am the first man to sit on top of the world." Henson said to him.

Peary checked his sextant again. Henson was right! The North Pole was within five kilometers (three miles). The next day, Peary took the team several miles beyond camp. They wanted to be sure they really touched the North Pole.

Bundled Up. *Henson wore this fur suit on his travels. It kept him warm at the icy, cold North Pole.*

Success! *Henson (center) and four Inuit members of the team stand with flags at the North Pole.*

Returning Home

Peary got bad news when they sailed home. Another man said he had reached the North Pole a year before. His name was Dr. Frederick Cook. People everywhere believed Cook.

Henson tried to tell the true story. Many people doubted a black man had reached the Pole. Finally, people learned Cook had lied. Peary became famous as the first one to reach the Pole. He received many honors.

Honoring Henson

At first, people remembered Henson as only a servant. Later, his true role became known. Congress gave him a medal. After his death, the National Geographic Society gave Henson its highest honor: a gold medal.

Today, the two explorers are buried side by side. There are words on Henson's grave. "The lure of the Arctic is tugging at my heart. To me, the trail is calling."

WORDWISE

Arctic Circle: area surrounding the North Pole

expedition: a long journey by a group of people to explore an area

navigation: helping by guiding one's way during travel

North Pole: the northernmost point of Earth's axis

South Pole: the southernmost point of Earth's axis

Race to the

Join two explorers as they ra

By Michael E. Ruane

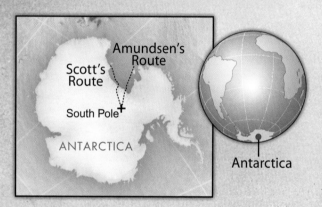

Amundsen's Route

Scott's Route

South Pole

ANTARCTICA

Antarctica

APONY WALKED through deep snow. Robert F. Scott watched it. It struggled to stay on its feet. It was winter in 1911. Scott was trying to reach the **South Pole**. He had tried once. Scott and his team came close on that expedition. But they didn't make it. This time he decided to take ponies. He took fewer sled dogs. Maybe that would help.

Two Men, One Goal

Roald Amundsen had the same goal. He led another expedition. Each of the men wanted to be the first person to reach the South Pole. It was a race to the Pole!

Each man's team would travel more than 2,900 kilometers (1,800 miles). One man would make it. The other would lose his life.

Getting Ready

The teams planned their trips. Scott would take the same path he had before. Amundsen would go through an unexplored area.

South Pole

to the bottom of the world.

Each team set up supply stations. The stations were along the paths the men would take. They left food and fuel for heat at them. That way they wouldn't have to carry many supplies.

Danger on the Ice

Disaster struck after setting up one of the supply stations. Some of Scott's sled dogs fell into a crack in the ice.

Scott's team was able to pull out most of the dogs. But they couldn't reach two of them.

Scott's team dropped a rope into the crack. Scott climbed down the rope. He grabbed the frightened dogs. He rescued them.

Better Sled. *A member of Amundsen's team works on a sled to make it slide easily on ice and snow.*

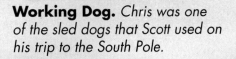

Working Dog. *Chris was one of the sled dogs that Scott used on his trip to the South Pole.*

Roald Amundsen of Norway. *Amundsen and his men look up at their country's flag at the South Pole.*

The Race Begins

AMUNDSEN: Spring came. Amundsen felt ready. He and his team loaded the sleds. The dogs pulled the sleds. The men skied beside them.

A blizzard struck. The team stayed calm. The men set up tents and cooked a meal. They fed the dogs.

SCOTT: Scott left his camp two weeks later. He hoped the ponies could survive in the cold.

Scott and his team felt cold. Their wool clothes did not keep them warm. The clothing took a long time to dry.

AMUNDSEN: Weeks passed. The dogs and the men were hungry.

They came to a large ice mountain. The dogs tried hard to pull the sleds. The ice was steep. They kept going.

SCOTT: Scott's team got stuck in a blizzard. They waited inside their tent.

The storm lasted four days. The ponies died. Scott's team had to pull the sleds.

Robert R. Scott of Great Britain. *Scott and his team reached the South Pole weeks after Amundsen.*

Spiky Shoes. *Scott's men wore shoes with spikes. The shoes helped them walk on ice.*

AMUNDSEN: Amundsen's men had frostbite on their hands and feet. The dogs were very hungry. They tried to eat a pair of boots.

Amundsen checked his navigation instruments one day. He was standing at the South Pole. His team had won!

SCOTT: Scott and his men were sick and weak. Scott saw a flag left behind by Amundsen one morning. He knew he had lost the race.

Scott's team had reached the Pole 34 days after Amundsen. They began the trip back. Another blizzard struck. The team could not go on.

Recovery Mission

A rescue party found Scott's tent months later. He and his team had died of hunger and cold.

Scott and Amundsen are still remembered today. Their courage inspires others. Brave explorers continue to go on dangerous expeditions. They make discoveries that amaze us all.

Real Gear. *Scott's team used these skis and sled.*

Reach Your Goals

Follow the race to the Poles. Then answer these questions.

1. What skills did the Inuit teach Henson?

2. How did Henson help make the journey to the North Pole a success?

3. Why did Scott and Amundsen race to the South Pole?

4. How did Scott and Amundsen prepare for their trips?

5. What two questions do you have about the trips to the Poles? Where can you look to find the answers?